# .....DEDICATIONS.....

## Paisley and Liam

You mean **everything** to me. You both give me a reason to write. You both give me a reason to find the beauty in the littlest and simplest of things. I hope you get everything you want out of life. I hope half of these poems, never make any sense to you. Finally, I hope you only ever have peace and love in your life.

## Mom

For always believing that I could do what I set my mind to and for being my biggest supporter/role mode, since day one. You have helped me get through some of the darkest times in my life. I love you! Thank you for always being someone I can count on no matter what. Finally, thank you for getting me through all of the death and chaos in my life.

# TABLE OF CONTENTS

# TABLE OF CONTENTS

# Up

Church bells ringing,
Playing hymns into the night,
Soft small child.
Why do you lay with eyes of red?
The cross YOU bear.
Lifts us up,
Up, up, up, from hell.
Like a toy meant for you,
Kiss your mother now before you go!
Up, up, up to heaven.
Singing "We are one,"
You call me your daughter,
Though, like I, a child you still are.
Take me up, up, up to the heavens.
Church bells ringing,
Playing hymns into the night.

## Desert love

4  Ring the bell rung,
    Music to my ears.
    The song has been sung,
19 The melody is what everyone hears.
    The fields of flowers live,
    Nature is destroyed pride.
    Hanging off the low give,
39 Leaving the rivers to become dry.
    Tears of the trees of fire,
    Your warm smile melts my heart.
    You alone are a friendly liar,
64 We are one and will never part.

<u>Stacked Deck</u>
Nobody has it, but it is everyone desire
Green and gray flying through the air throughout
Digging holes into the hearts of loved ones
Waking the world with loud cries and greed.

It doesn't speak, but it yells louder than us
Demanding our love, our main attention
Seeking the path of the buyer beware
Forcing our hand, cards we haven't been dealt.

The love we share is too great for us both
Giving you away is no easy task
But keeping you close is getting harder to bear
Nothing stays forever. This, too, shall pass.

When the broken wealth of the world yells,
You play your hand and bluff.

## Daily rush
Holding hands walking in,
A father, a daughter from the south.
Old and young with coffees in hand,
Lattes up next!
It's ours! It's ours! With giggles flying,
A broken crumble of food scattered amongst papers.
They are friends at work,
Running, running, worker bees working.
Air rushes in, pushing cups to fly.
Old and young, frustrated and waiting.
The jitters that spread from hand to heart,
Coffee is lacking though it is all around,
Sugar grains spread like sand on a beach,
With puddles of milk as big as the ocean waves.
Lovers walk through to have the same,
Love overheating, with drinks burning mouths all the same.

### *Assume Nothing*

Assumptions are a threat,
Holding the truth among the lies,
Having the steak at the mouth of a hungry wolf,
Holding a gasoline-soaked match to a flame.

Assumptions are a tolerance trap,
Without A, you cannot possibly have B,
Without a line, you cannot catch the fish,
Without a thought, you have no plan.

Assumptions are misleading,
At the thought of being told the truth,
At the hand of a trusted lover,
At the end of the barrel of a gun.

Assumptions are necessary,
With a child holding a mother's hand crossing a street,
With a kiss between fighting lovers making up,
With a test studied for days before, hoping to pass.

Assumptions are what they are,
Like a red bird on fire.

## Sunny Frozen Love

Baby, we can reach the sun,
The sun will kiss your soft lips,
Burning holes in the heart.
Nothing feels wrong now.
We were born from the sun,
Set my lips on fire,
Kiss them till they are charred black,
Hold me with fire eyes.
A blazing heart on ice,
Melt me down to the sweet,
Puddles, puddles forming,
The world is falling too.
Pieces on the ground crack,
Baby, we have reached the sun,
The sun kissed your soft lips.

_____High as a wire_____

The bird flies with a broken wing,
Leaving its feathers to change color,
Her majestic beak forming into a sword,
Singing its song of love taking away your pain.

Remembering a life that once was,
Eating worms, flying wire high,
Until colors flooded its wings,
It can be all things, see all sights.

The loved one's tears lift it higher up,
Ascending to the heavens where birds lay at rest,
All changing form, resounding in colors.
Red and blue, green and yellow, orange and purple, forming.

Peace of the mind sending waves of laughter,
Love in the heart holding the child's hand,
Greed when the man-made hope is pricier,
Happiness is when you become a bird of unimaginable colors.

Evolution
The infant lay cold,
Holding the silver lining, growing old,
The boys sing songs of destruction and death,
Oh, what a joy to be young, such new breath.


Abstract Resolution
Adding color into a puzzling world,
Twists and turns surround every dimly lit area,
A love brought out the darkest of lies ever spoke,
(4)     This is a place of chaos and destruction, too.

Familiar is not a friend, but a common shape,
Bringing together jagged edges to make sense,
A puzzle you can't jam the pieces to make fit,
(8)     Ancient time of love and war, a tragic disaster.

Friends at a table leave a somber feeling,
Laughing and drinking all is fine in the world,
Red, black, green, yellow, blue, and grey with a pinch of white,
(12)    Leaving the darkness to surround the edges here.

A savior with a rope, mapping out shame like clouds,
Hoping to find peace amongst the rubble of fear,
(15)    Where friendship once was; destruction, death, and chaos are near.


_____ *Trails*
We walk together side by side,
Nowhere to go, nothing to hide.
Your hand in mine, walking together,
No matter what, we are forever.
My heart is yours, and yours is mine,
We lose ourselves when our minds intertwine.
The smile you have that sparkles like snow,
Leaving the heart with nothing left but to grow.
Your kiss leaves my lips warm from the fire,
Withholding the pain of the wanted desire.
We walk together side by side,
Nowhere to go, nothing to hide.

Sun Kisses

I can feel the sun touch my soft lips,
It doesn't burn, but it tingles instead.
The air around whispers lovely stories,
Leaving you guessing as to how it will end.

The clouds roll in, and lightning strikes the ground,
Flowers on fire left crying in the dirt.
Unable to move, the sun runs away,
Leaving its branded mark on my burnt lips.

The aftermath is ash with flower tears,
My skin is just a vessel for the sun now.
I hear the trees singing the song of air,
On repeat, in my heart, it does echo.

"Never was a love so dry. The sun is out,
To say goodbye, leaving another lie."

## Eternity changed

*The day is new, but you're still the same*
*Your heart is still whole but shattered all out on the floor*
*Not knowing what to say or do*
*The only thing you can muster is a blank stare into the void*
*You feel together yet separated from your body all at once*
*Nothing is the same*
*Everything is changed*
*You went from perfect to impractical in a matter of days*
*You don't know how to tell up from down and left from right*
*Sad songs, sad movies, sad quotes make more sense*
*Are you just pretending happiness, or is it real?*
*Nothing will be the same again*
*Everything has changed forever*
*In the blink of an eye.*

## THROUGH THE PAIN

The words flew up in the air,
Hearts are broken without care,
The scars were left in plain sight,
We all knew it wasn't right.

Nobody said a positive word,
But not one person was even heard,
There's never a pain that cuts as deep,
As for the thickest of blood, it did seep.

My tears filled with only regret,
Wishing we had never met,
Your words cut more profoundly than a knife,
I wish I lived another life.

The thoughts flooded through my head,
I wanted to run and hide under my bed,
I saw a mirror of a girl happy as could be,
Deep down, I knew the girl was me.

# Fragrance

she swore up and down
never again
 the sheets were still white
her body remained intact
 but her heart remained at the bottom of the glass
sitting on a bar stool
 hours in the past
drinking away the memories of what lay ahead
 years before it caught up to her
the smell of his cologne drew her in
 like brie cheese to a cultured mouse
the mouse never learned
 one day the trap would be set
being told no was never going to work
 maybe the next time the bar stool called
shed swear never again, again.

## Jesus A Son

Church bells ringing,
Playing hymns into the light,
Soft small child.
Why do you wake with eyes of red?
The pain you endured,
Lifts them up.
Up, up, up from hell.
Like a song meant just for you,
Wave to your father now when you arrive.
Up, up, up to heaven.
Swimming in the sea of the blue sky,
Continued singing "we are one."
With sounds of voices marching through the air,
You call me your son.
Though, like I, you are a child too.
Take me up to the heavens,
Up, up with all of your might.
The ringing of the bells,
Stopping after the morning light rises.

# EVIL OF TONIGHT

LUST IS LUST LEAVING THE HEART TO BE FREE,

THE CROSS YOU BEAR REPRESENTS THE PAST VERSION OF YOU,

A DOVE SO WHITE THE PAINT IS JEALOUS,

FIRE SPREAD WHEN YOU SPOKE, LEAVING ONLY ASH,

ASHES TO ASHES, HEART TO HEART, YOU SAY,

BUT YOU BURNT THE HEART INTO BLACK TAR,

HOLDING YOUR HAND, WALKING WITH THE TRUE DEVIL,

NOT KEEPING MY HAND TO YOUR HEART, TO LIES,

LIES SPOKEN IN THE NIGHTLY SHADE GIVEN,

DEAMONS SPRING FROM THE BED AND INTO MY SOUL,

SQUEEZING MY LIFE AS WELL AS MY LOVE,

GRIPPING MY HEART WITH SWEET LIES OF TONIGHT,

AS I BREATHE, THEY BREATHE,

THE EVIL IS INSIDE OUT NOW,

I SEE WITH LUST-FILLED EYES THAT YOU ARE FREE.

# wind

The wind is, but a strange friend
It shelters itself around us
To protect us from its path
It leaves unheard whispers floating above
It can be as cold as ice
Or as hot as a flame burning ever so bright
But it never goes; it only stands still
Playing a game of freeze tag in the light
The wind can change your mind
But never your fate
It reaches out a hand to lead you where you are meant to go
Gently brushing against your cheek
Telling no lies or hiding from you
Swiftly, like a blade swaying by
Or slow as a heartbeat when fading to peace
Nothing can take the wind away
Except for you

SEASONS
I hate being here,
It is spring, not summer time,
The sun shines air flows.

I want to eat fruit,
In a bikini, I go.
Burning my skin off.

Criminal, my life.
Winter time is my best friend,
No sun, anyway.

The world escapes me,
In the breeze of the spring air,
Driving to hell's gate.

SEASONS II
Being anywhere in the summer time,
The spring first before the dawn.
The sun is shining the air flows around.

Fruit is the friend we knew and lost,
Swimming a day to pass the time,
Lost love of mine like a fire with no flame.

I steal your love with a kiss,
In the snow on your shoe,
Leaving footprints to unmask the summer we once saw.

The world is unknown to me.
Remembering, the love we once knew and understood,
It leads us away from pain into the heart of the cage.

Tranquility

She looked from a distance
Scared to dip her toes in the dark ocean
The smell lured her in
The feeling was enticing
Yet she never got too close
Not knowing what she was afraid of
Only knowing she was afraid
Day after day
Closer and closer
One day
The sun beat down on the ocean
The water, impossible to resist
Nothing would stop her
Her toes went in
Then her foot
Then her ankle
Then her leg
Suddenly she was submerged
The fear washed away
She felt whole
At peace

# EXPERIMENT 0923

It is messy
It is toxic
A science experiment gone wrong
We are the villains
In this superhero-filled world
Passionate, of course
Dysfunctional at best
Bombs always exploding
Maniacal laughter evolved from pain
We know which landmines to avoid
And when to pull the trigger
On the roulette loaded gun
There is no cure in the end
No hero waiting to save you from yourselves
Only beautiful wreckage
And chaos
I wouldn't want it any other way
Just us
And the bombs.

RECHARGEABLE BATTERY

    Bruises heal

    Scratches fade

    A piece of me is taken away

    Thrown into the water, unable to swim,

    Drowning in the ocean of black

    Unable to breathe like a pillow,

    Trapped within a sheet

    Tears flow, and then they stop

    Were the bruises real?

    Were the scratches not that deep?

    Was I crazy?

    Smile. Wave. Lie.

    It's a new day

    a new slate

        The roses look beautiful on the table

INTO THE RING
The gloves were almost glued to his hands
They never came off
She gave them as a gift
A gift for loving her
Round after round
Until his fingers bled
His knuckles blood stained callouses
Resembling that of a marble statue
He took them off when she left the ring
When the hollow cube was empty,
When no competitor would show their face
She showed up at the ring
Flickering of lights
Nobody around
Day after day until the last
The glow had almost gone
A box in the center of the ring
Spreading hope
Spreading anticipation
Only to find a gift for her
A gift for loving him
The gloves

Spring Sun

The sun is faded
Yet the air feels fresh and clean
The grass dead, not green


Spring Bloom
Flowers, flowers everywhere
The wind is messing up my hair
Spring yet, fully sprung


Boom
The sun
The deer feces
Your gun

Favorite color

SHE LOVED THE COLOR RED

NOBODY KNEW

THE SHADE WAS JOYFUL

IT WAS KIND

IT WAS PASSIONATE

RED WAS NEVER THE SAFE OPTION

SHE DREW WITH IT IN SECRET

IT WAS ALL THE WONDERFUL ASPECTS

BUT ALSO, WRONG

ANGER AND HEARTBREAK

SHE LOVED THE COLOR BLUE

IT WAS ALL SHE WAS GIVEN

THE SHADE WAS DARK

IT WAS STRONG

IT WAS SAFE

BLUE WAS AS SAFE AS IT GOT

IT BROUGHT HER CLOSER TO THE OCEAN

SHE USED IT ALL THE TIME

IT WAS GREAT THINGS

BUT ALSO, EXPECTED

WOEFUL AND DESPERATION

# Run your race

She gets angry

Her eyes want to release a flood onto the ground

Creating an ocean so massive it covers the planet

Her breathing hastens

She feels as if she were running a race

She was winning

But she wanted desperately to lose

She untied her shoes, hoping to trip

To land on the ground, unable to move

To lose.

She wanted desperately to lose.

Her thoughts raced and stopped in the back of her mind

If you spoke, she didn't hear

You're a mouth moving in front of her eyes

You lie.

You hold her hand, sending love into her ears

You tied her shoes and sent her on

Watching a smile go to her cheeks,

She says sorry

She feels sorry and insists you're both fine

You're both going to be fine

She lied.

Oh, She got first place.

___Mirror|rorriM___
The skin she wore felt like it wasn't hers at all
It was as if she had been wearing a heavy winter coat
In the middle of summer
With stones in the pockets
The tie around the center meant to be decoration
Hugged her so tight her lungs gasped
Resembling a fish out of water. She was drowning.
Sending a panic down her spine, making her feel cold
Then feel guilt.
She looked at the coat and couldn't take it off before bed
Before a shower
Mad at the reflection, hating the stranger staring at her
Screaming out, "WHY? WHY THIS JACKET?"
This wasn't even her color; it was never meant for her to wear
It was a gift
A gift to herself she didn't mean to order
Shipping took months; she forgot it was ordered at all
But once it arrived, she tried it on
It was stuck to her.
The compliments stopped
The favors had stopped
The guilt grew until it consumed her
She had nowhere left to turn but to sink
She sank further into the jacket

## Thoroughbred

There was a day I could run,
Wild and free,
The wild side in me is deep down and bare,
My hair growing, and I am new to the world.

I sit with Mama and Daddy there too,
Then shots come around in the dead of night,
Daddy screams, "Stop!" and with one blow to the head,
There's no more sickness for Mama.

My mouth shut tight.
Crying in the night for them,
Why would they do that?
Why would they just take my family away?

They say I am worth thousands,
I can run fast and am to be a *brute of a stallion*,
They want to brand me their own,
"You can't keep me tied down," but they don't listen.

I try to tell them to leave me alone,
The child they produce will grow big and strong,
He won't be a stranger,
They want me to befriend him.

"A horse for you, Jimmy,"
They say, "Look what we bought!"
"We bought him from town,"
"He is all yours and your responsibility now."

I give in to friendship,
The boy Jimmy ain't bad,
He gave me some hay in the morning, at least,
He even brushes my mane.

At night I feel sad,
When I'm all alone,
I wish Mama and Daddy were here,
And could see me now.

There was a day I could run,
Wild and free,
The wild side in me is deep down and bare
My hair grew, and I feel as if I am new to the world.

# Let Go

The pain filled my heart and my soul.
I couldn't let her go,
Not yet; I'm not ready.
I wear the symbol of you on a chain,
And I hold you dear in my heart,
You might be gone, but you are still here.
I feel you looking and smiling on any occasion,
Your look of disapproval when something isn't quite right,
I don't care what happens, but I care what you see.
I try to do the best I can,
To make you proud,
Your love fills my heart and gives me the strength.
It runs through my veins and sets you free,
You are in every action and live on through me,
I let you go, but keep your love within my heart and soul.

## ~~untethered~~

Games upon games we play,
We laugh in the sun's glimmering ray.
My heart is a slate, clean and dry,
All throughout the world, in space and time.
The water deeper, than a tear that falls,
The pain of tomorrow, it still calls.
I never want to be alone,
With a blade, fully grown.
A sharpened thought that runs free,
Leaving you left to only see.
I am blind and scared of sight,
People kill for what's in the light.
A fear of death I have never known,
Until your love, a gun was shown.
Your blanket around me is safe and secure,
We are what we are and not what we were.
You hate to love and love to destroy,
My heart is the game, and my love, the toy.
I grabbed the gun; you lit a match,
Your plan is working, seeming to hatch.
I loved once and twice in the sun,
But three times no more, our love is done.
You forget the gun while you sleep,
Leaving me to only weep.
Through eyes that are blind, beginning to see,
The holder now of love is me.
You beg, "Don't shoot," and I cry out in pain,
The boom goes off, just like your name.
A flower withered; a river run dry,
My hand of blood and my eyes that cry.
I loved you then; I love you still,
I will love you forever, forever until.

*Without Pain*

The sky lit with a shiny glow,
The doves flew high and swooped low,
The grass swayed left and right,
Never letting go, the love of the night.

My heart and mind are calm as rain,
Having nothing left to obtain,
In the end, they were all there,
But all that's left is a single prayer.

A teary-eyed child whispers a plea,
"Please let there be no pain and let her be free,
They say when you're gone, it's a safe place,
So please stay with her and fill her with grace."

I saw him plea with God for me,
If only it were possible for him to see,
My pain is gone, and I am clear,
Do not cry for me, young boy; I am always near.

*Innocence*

The smile left by the rose
Is but a humble sound.
There is no crime in the thorns,
Only a whisper of hearts.
A wave crashing upon a sandy open shore,
No longer shark-infested waters.
The pain at the end of the night,
Shrieking into my legs through my mouth.
Like worms crawling in and out of a corpse,
Holding dirt in my hand and tossing it down.
The water has risen, and the leaves are withered,
A rose, ever so pure, so red, so flourished.
No more.
The sound of the ocean beaming from ear to ear.
There is no one to listen,
There is nothing to hear now, only the breeze.

Abandonment
    A. ttention not given
    B. ottling up emotions
    A. ltering of the mind
    N. obody is there for you
    D. eath of the soul
    O. wning unnecessary responsibility
    N. obody cares
    M. oments of heartache
    E. go damaging
    N. ot being good enough
    T. he responsible victim

*Blue Bird*

The fire lit within her toes
And within the depths, an angel rose
Her soul rose up into the black of night
She had a lot left in her, a lot of fight.

Her white wings embedded inside of her back
It felt as if lightning struck with a mighty whack
The ashes of the stars burning so bright
Sent forth a tiny halo of the starry night.

She flew up as far as she could
Thinking she may be misunderstood,
The heavens opened up a voice called out:
"Fly in with only love and never a doubt."

The songs being sung she had never heard
In front of her flying was a little blue bird
God spoke to the angel. With much love, he did intend.
"Go forth, my child, and fly with your blue feathered friend."

## Please don't forget to forget me

I hope that when I die
Nobody's there at the funeral
I wish days go by
Nights drag on
Life continues as usual.

I hope everyone smiles
Laughter fills rooms
I hope everyone
Is eating
Out of their silver spoons.

I hope tears never fall
My phone never rings
I hope the only
Sounds are
When the child sings.

I hope mine don't miss me
I hope they forget
The person I was
The one
I wish they had never met.

I hope all of my pain
Is gone like the wind
I hope this never ends
Just like...

_____ *Beautiful Disasters.*

The way it feels is like a mountain crashing down at supersonic speed,

Watching the rocks fall above you with your rope secure against you. Knowing one,

　　　Will strike like a snake, but never know which one.

It feels like the start of a fantastic movie, but in the end, the dog dies in a fire.

　　　Blazing amongst the trees glowing bright orange.

The smoke left behind fills your lungs, tears swell up, and you lose the ability.

　　　To breathe.

Functioning becomes too much to bear, and you hope death happens faster or

　　　All at once.

It feels like a sailboat on top of the ocean in the middle of a hurricane.

You cling to the wheel, knowing it won't do anything other than balance you.

　　　Before the waves take over and crash down above you.

Dragging you down into the deepest, darkest parts of the ocean with nothing to look at

　　　In the blackest of blue waters and salt burns holes in your throat and stings,

　　　Your eyes more than your tears ever could.

The anchor tied around your foot dragging you further and further down. Knowing,

　　　You chose to sail, and only now when there is no hope, regret.

　　　Regret finally sets in.

Loving you is like choosing to go on a great adventure, only to die in the end in a

　　　Beautiful Disaster

## ETERNAL LOVE

One day when we're old and gray,
Nothing will be left to say.
Hearts beating side by side,
Nothing left to let slide by.
Our breaths both growing shallow and weak;
Nothing left but what seems so bleak.
The memories of a love that fit like a glove,
Are held close from up above.
God has said, "I give you both a love so strong,
That nothing could ever go so wrong.
You're close at heart or hand in hand,
No matter what or where you both stand."
Holding hands, they fall asleep,
Seeing the memories of which they keep.
Of a time so soft and so new,
When all their love began and grew.

## Soul catcher

They say the eyes are the windows to the soul.

If they were the windows, then the music you listen to bears no semblance to your emotions and individuality.

If they were the windows, the clothes you wear as expression are just but a fashion statement and not a need to show everyone how you feel inside and wear that around like a badge for all to see. To be made proud.

The morals you hold at the highest of value are just that of what you have been brainwashed to believe, the ideals that will get you to the finish line of what your parents believed the afterlife to be, and their parents before them and their parents before them and their parents before them…

The eyes are not windows to the soul; they are the microphone. Making it loud enough for the people in the back to hear; the quietest whisper that you can't even manage to say out loud, for fear they will hear too much.

They allow others to see into your heart, mind, and body with just one drop of water.

One wrinkle going upwards, shows an entire life that has far exceeded childhood and, sometimes, one that never had a childhood at all.

The eyes are not windows to the soul,
They are the soul.

## Say Cheese

*You can't make them see you the way that you do.*
*They see a photo.*
*A photo of sunshine on your face,*
        *The happiest person alive.*
*The smile that says:*
        *"I have made it in the world, and I. Am. Here!"*
*No.*
*They simply do not see.*
*Certainly not the moments leading up to that flash sending your eyes to see the stars,*
        *Briefly making you feel like a hollowed corpse and alone.*
*Certainly not the moments after when that smile dims.*
*Just for a second, as the flash disappears, and the raised eyebrows give way to the truth.*
*For just a split second,*
        *you forget the act you were portraying.*
*For just a split second,*
        *It wasn't an act.*
*Only you hold the mirror in front of your face at all times.*
*With all the tears flowing down like waterfalls, leaving oceans,*
        *The bottom is filled with boulders, not rocks.*
*The mirror,*
        *That shows the scars on your heart from the words spoken,*
*The thoughts,*
        *In your mind, made out of fear.*
*The damage,*
        *Of the wreckage behind you,*
        *That only surfaces when you look in that same mirror,*
        *Watching them whisper behind your shoulder, pointing at*
*The debris.*
*They gather around you as there is another flash.*
        *Don't forget to put the mirror down for Just. One. Moment,*
*Smile.*

July
You were born
The sun shines
Time to wake

December
You were born
The snow falls
Time to sleep

August
You did die
Child toy broke
Time to cry

## ~~Depression~~

Depression is a silent killer,
It cuts you like a knife,
You lose all sense of self,
You gain no state of life.

As you sulk in bed and cry,
Nothing left of hope,
You turn to the bottle,
As you begin to choke.

You feel alive when you're unaware,
Unconsciousness is your friend,
You'd much rather displace your fears,
Your morals will soon start to bend.

The drugs, they come too easy.
Feeling it with every pop,
Once a month to thrice a day,
You think you just can't stop.

You drink too much one night,
You feel dizzy and spin out,
The car lights fade into the dark,
You have taken the wrong route.

The surrounding alarms blaring in a daze,
Red and blue lights flashing,
With all the buzzing in your ear,
Your life continues crashing.

Your breathing slows enough,
The buzz you had is absent,
You return to your old senses,
The depression begins its harassment.

*You put the bottle to your lips,*
*With tears down your face,*
*The bottle of pills consumed,*
*The world is not your place.*

*You grab the bottle lying in the tub,*
*You can't help but feel alone,*
*You do what you have always done,*
*This is all you have been shown.*

*You vomit down your chest,*
*Drink more to wash it down,*
*It will soon be in the papers,*
*It will be throughout the town.*

*Your eyes flutter shut,*
*Your breathing becomes weak,*
*A smile spread across your face,*
*If only you knew, you could speak.*

*Depression is a silent killer,*
*It cuts you like a knife,*
*You lose all sense of self,*
*You gain no state of life.*

# Time

I set everything around you.
Ever since the beginning,
Without you my world would fall apart.
I wouldn't know where to go,
I wouldn't know when to start.
My movies would have no beginning,
Songs would have no end.
Birthdays,
Holidays,
Dates,
Nothing would matter.
Routine would cease,
Breakfast lunch and dinner would simply be only words.
The things I enjoy would not exist,
The world would turn upside down.
The ocean would dry up and the sun would go out.
Like a candle,
But instead of wind there is only a void.
A dark and endless void, inside of my mind,
Inside of my heart.
But time exists in this world,
And only time, will tell.

# Flame

His heart was warm when she sat near
Like sitting next to a campfire
He was, in fact, her match,
And her the gasoline.

They burned bright together.
Made an engulfed forest fire look insignificant
The forest fire appeared as small as an ant,
Under a microscope, under the blazing sun.

Her gasoline lead for miles in a trickle
Waiting patiently in an ocean of fumes,
Waiting for her match to light,
To ignite a flame.

When it did
It hurt
It felt amazing
It felt
cold.

Matches only burn for so long.

ISBN: 979-8-9884961-0-6 (paperback)

www.ingramcontent.com/pod-product-compliance
Lightning Source LLC
LaVergne TN
LVHW080054090426
835513LV00031B/1237